Soft Touch Of Passion's Flame

Soft Touch Of Passion's Flame

Marshall A. Azir

Cover by
John Deric G. Domingo
johnderic.g.domingo@gmail.com

Interior Design by
Diana Lyn G. Domingo
dianne.g.domingo@gmail.com
and
Miaca Elizabelle A. Contemplacion
miacaelizabelle08@gmail.com

Hiwaga
PUBLISHING

DEDICATION

These poems are dedicated to the passion of feeling hearts touch. We so often want to dedicate our words to someone. I seek to dedicate this to the infinite cycle of our seasons of passions when they touch us and when they don't.

ACKNOWLEDGMENTS

I would like to thank the following:

Hiwaga Publishing, Inc.

Janice De Jesus

Stephanie Licudine

All the experiences that brought these passions into a soft touch of words

CONTENTS

SOFT TOUCH

HOLD YOU

I should have told you.

Let me hold you,

Braiding your intimate imitations into idyllic imagery

Let me hold you,

Associating our attraction to astronomy; Astronomical
    units acceding in our Auras

Let me hold you,

Creating an earthquake of emotion; Elapsing time
    caused by our eclipse of miscommunication

Let me hold you,

Putting your hand in mine, matching energies,
    magnetically molding our marrow

Let me hold you,

Joining our jostled reality, justice being a journey to
    this moment

Let me hold you,

While you hold me

THE COMPLEXITY OF US

We have been compounding interest of desire,
My craving for your heart has been a high APR,
Leaving us in a lover's debt

Sadly, we have been nerds,
Trying to balance the perfect equation of opportunity
    but left empty,
Never sharing our heart's findings, leaving us ignorant
    of our joint truth,
Leaving us to form the worse conspiracy, What if…
Many won't understand the similes and metaphors of
    our math science,
But the fact you do leaves me orbiting a divine
    celestial body,
Craving to enter your sincere atmosphere.

Do you understand?
The thought of our equal but never opposite desire is a
    supermassive gravity well,
Causing my galaxy to rotate around you

The mass of our attraction is so heavy it has two
    moons
You,
Me,
Holding us in dual orbit around the things that pull us
    together,
The sad part about it,
Someone has always been on the dark side,
Unable to retrograde in orbit,
Someone has always been close to the limit,
    but we are asymptotes,
Because the integrations of our desires have never
    met,
Hidden behind the finite barrier between us,
It's just the square root of a negative one because
    no matter how I imagine things together
It only conjugates itself, never affecting the root
When will this complexity untangle itself?

LET ME TOUCH YOU

Let me hold your hands,

Feeling the delicate, precious nature of your touch

Let me hold your eyes,

Diving deep into windows of your essence

No longer lingering in pain at the pane

Let me hold your lips,

Pressing soft curves of your sweetness against my

      perception of taste

Tasting the luscious gentle origin of your voice

Hoping to savor the sip of your beautiful connection of

      senses

Let me hold your body,

Feeling the warmth of the hottest rising wind,

Becoming your meteorologist

Predicting humid rainy seasons

Holding your whole-body embrace

Let me hold your hair,

Tangling me in the garden of your fertile thoughts and

    hopes

Holding your pride and joy,

Cherishing the work you put in,

Cause no matter its shape, it's continually blossoming

Shining in my eyes to the world around you

Let me hold your laugh,

Feeling the joy of your spirit in mine,

Saturating joy in my heart with the happiness in yours

Desiring always to see your eyes filled with delight

Hanging on to your jokes like the best episode of a

    stand-up,

Having to pause because you take my breath away

Let me hold your passion,

Firing up true feelings when I hold your hands

Igniting the friction of desires,

Shocking us into the wave of thought,

We belong together, on all layers

Let me hold your kisses,

Holding on to the small notes of your exquisite melody

Listening with my lips instead of my ears,

Nibbling at supple dreams, our lips in contact

Let me hold your caresses,

Reviving the dream deferred

Cascading into the kinetic shock of a decade-long

      curious craving

Let me hold your dreams,

Watering the seeds of your greatness,

Most of all, let me hold you,

All of you

Together

Because that's all I ever wanted

You and me, all together

YEARNING

I woke up,

You weren't there

I get out of bed,

Your voice I didn't hear

I walked out the door,

Your touch I didn't feel

I got in the car,

Your presence wasn't there to heal

SHOULD'VE KISSED YOU

I should have kissed you

And now I dream of you

Which has left me dearly departed

Wishing to be again open-hearted

I should've kissed you

Tasting all the elements of your desire

I should've kissed you

Sealing our connection with a tangible token

I should've kissed you

Touching you with magical machinations of yearning

I should've kissed you

Sampling your delightful smile

I should've kissed you

Showing our desire is a kinetic pulse,

Flowing through your body

Sending shock waves of rippled passion

I should've kissed you

Holding your mind, body and spirit

Uniting our attraction with reality

One where more than our lips meet

But our souls weave into an intimate braid

WISHING LANGUAGE

I wish I could speak your language

But I don't know Japanese

I wish I could speak your love language,

But I don't know how to sculpt clay

I wish I could speak tantalizing haikus

But I can only watch you

I wish I could whisper wishful words

In your sweet, delicate ears

Telling you how much I want to glide my hands

     around your form

I wish I could show you how I can sculpt,

Not with clay

But with words and hands

I can re-sculpt your body with these mahogany hands

Sliding them down your sides with a tender touch,

Grabbing delicate spots with care

If I were to sculpt a figurine

It would be you with me,

Golden breasts will always shape and reshape

Perfectly cut proportions

Hair swoops and relaxes in the perfectly precise
     location

My hands desire to mold us together

And fire us in the oven of desire

Showing when we touch each other

It leaves deep impressions on both of us

Let's be artwork

No matter how much clay is on your hand,

They will be clean in my heart

Place your hands on me

So, you can lay the foundation of our bodies,
     sculpting the perfect image of us

BELOVED

Over the top

Under the bottom

The tastes of honey

Sweet to the touch

Stick to the heart

She is honey, slowly leaving my thoughts

Can the wind blow this way again?

Passion is a fruit saturating me with its juices

In the palm tree of sweetness

Her legs

The smooth

Sleek

Touch of beloved legs

SOFT TOUCHES

Soft touch of Dreaming Gleam

Your touch a tender addiction

Warm eyes, shining in sun ray stream

Your morning gaze dream's dictation

My dear your smile

Is the fuel for intimacy's fire

Enriching my hope to stay awhile

The glow of your being, love's choir

Your essence calls out to my deep

Speaking to my inner core

If the world collapsed, you I'd keep

In you I infinitely pour

My lover, friend and confidante

May we remain bonded all lifetime

Let our pasts no longer haunt

In time souls will embrace affection's prime.

MELODIES OF INTIMACY

Eighty-eight keys unlock a piano's melody,

Yet, what unlocks your intimacy?

Chords of focused love languages,

Can interlock souls,

But how does one braid togetherness deeper?

How do two separate cultures come into one?

How do black and white extremes

Come together to make songs and riffs?

How does frayed chaos

Come to braided intimacy?

When does Me flip,

Becoming We?

How does the discord of US

Come together and make music?

When do broken notes,

Become streams of sweet sound?

When does misunderstanding,

Become more than a speed bump,

But the mechanism to intertwine deeper?

Many want to translate love to intimacy,

Without having basic heart grammar

The syntax of sensuality is a certificate of appreciation

Leaving us to wonder is there a degree with

     more meaning

The depths of intimacy,

A smile and a tear

A smile, shining soothing symmetries on our hearts

A tear, titrating tension in the core of our earnest

     intentions

The melody of intimacy

Is grammar of the heart,

Our deepest desires yearning to communicate

Our bad grammar producing broken or run-on

     sentences,

Leaving others to hear a broken note

Making us realize we need rehearsals

Rehearsing what it means to be felt accurately

MEMORY MOON

The thoughts of you orbit,
Reminding me the value of joint laughter

The dreams of you pull me,
Rippling moments of precious eye contact

The visions of you shine on me,
Brightening my countenance from your soft touch

You are no longer my moon
I release you to a new system

What we share are memories
Embers of reality
We can daydream about ancient almost treasuries,,
Allowing our unforgettable potential energy
      to turn into a banshee

But there is no need to haunt

Only release

Releasing the want,

Is the best way for us to live in peace

Take care Moon of Magnificent Memories

May you be blessed by a warm life filled planet.

PASSION'S FLAME

TEW

She is art

Touch her

She is music

Listen to her

She is water

I feel her

She is art

I gaze into her

She is music

I listen to her body

She is water

Be a part of her flow

She is art

I touch her

I whisper to her in the shower

I pierce her more than her piercings

I penetrate her deeper than the ink on her skin

She is music
I listen to her
Her body is open to me
I glide my hands down it
I feel clean with her touch

She is water
Wet when I'm here
Waiting for me to saturate her
And lather me with her essence
I hold her while I shower with her life

LEGS

Long lavish legs

My mesmerized mind

Long lavish legs

Imagination ignites inside

Long lavish legs

Sweet smell, savory

Long lavish legs

Carved continually, carefully

Long lavish legs

Soothing smooth surfaces

Long lavish legs

Lavished

Long

Legs

Thighs that sigh

To calves that caress

Long lavish legs

MOMENT LOVER

I would call her lover.

But she is on the dance floor

Moving with her salt-and-pepper hair

Seasoning my attraction with each movement

Marinating my daydreams

Wondering what it's like,

To caress her

To kiss her closely

I would call her lover.

But the dance floor separates us

Not in time, but in distance

Can we touch lips?

Can we touch bodies

Because the way she moves,

Is a fountain my youth wants to dip into.

I would call her lover,

But the dance floor is a wall, blocking.

I would call her lover,

But touching her is a poem, not reality

I would call her lover,

But Mrs. doesn't even know I exist.

BLACK MAMBA

I thought heavenly bodies could only be found in the
    sky
I was wrong

The melanin-rich soul before me proved me wrong
She is dark, thick and warm
Her body in savory positions
Black, on black, on black
Black painted nails
Black lipstick
Black skin
Fullness in moments
She moves her hips like an ancient spell
Each dip and rotation are incantations
I fall deeper into her cauldron of passion
Each level closer to her warmness
Gliding hands around her curves
Her curves deserve placated monuments
Because only divine beings can craft such things

She is a temple of divine craftmanship

Each curve softly caresses a nerve

She is a melanin queen, rich

And I only desire to dine with the queen

Or on the queen

Devouring the pink feast in her sea of melanin

Being showered with savory juices

A royal feast

I want to dive deep into her melanin treasury

Adding riches to her pink center

Only giving deposits of tongued currency

Oh, to plunge into the bank of fertile soil

Is it passion to know how a heavenly body can touch a

    mortal such as me?

THEM

I love them

Affection and articulation are appointed to them

Rave radiating reverence romance them

Even engaging eagerness enables ensuing exaltation

Oh, oval oasis overflow with my obsession

Lust lingers, longing for large lucid limits

Analytical and artistic admiration absorb into them

Surely said, such softness is a sacrament for sexual

    salvation

I love them

SHE WAKES IN ELEGANCE

She wakes in elegance, like a star

Her cinnamon hue absorbing rays of light

Morning brightness saturating her image without mar

Curves accenting the brown sight

She is covered in perfection, contained in a tender jar

A true manifestation of beauty's might

The morning sun gleaning down from beyond

Shining on her brown sugar thighs

Thick sweet goodness solidifying desires bond

Her gaze, a place where fear dies

Yet, her face, a place where beauty and passion find

Lines and curves form her being, showing her creator
    wise

Slender and curved, a perfect mixture

It hypnotizes the watchful duo in my face

My neck becoming stiff, a focused fixture

Forever devoted to the celestial beauty captured in the
    cinnamon case

My dreams could never picture

A more gorgeous human vase

CONTRAST

I love it when you hold me

When our skin touches

My heart pounds into submission

We are artists, our very contrast in skin proves it

Your light hue touches my dark hue

We are a perfect mixed medium

Hold my darkness

As I embrace your brightness

Onyx and ivory

I love the contrast

When you hold me with your pale hands,

I am saturated with love

When your blue eyes gaze into mine

I am electrified with desire

When your soft pink lips touch mine,

I am disarmed, lowering my heart's defense

When I feel your savory milky body next to mine

I am high, off the contrast color

When I hold your thighs in my hands

I am hypnotized by the feeling

When I hold on to your creamy-colored ass

I am enchanted by its shape

When I nibble on your coral-colored nipples

I am mesmerized by the aroma

When I slide into your delicate flushed walls

I am fulfilled by the in-depth contrast

The dark, entering the light for passionate pleasure

You and I are art

Your pinks and whites

My browns and tans

We are a masterpiece untamed

Carved in shaded ambition

PLEASE AND THANK YOU

Please...

Your eyes yearn for warm touch

I look into them longing for sweet embrace

Thank You

Please...

Our bodies know the mood

Our eyes speak tepid tensions

Our hands reach for material passion

Thank You

Please...

Kiss me in ways I never knew

Touch me in places I feel tender

Taste me in forms I always wanted

Appreciate me in methods I call out for

Thank You...

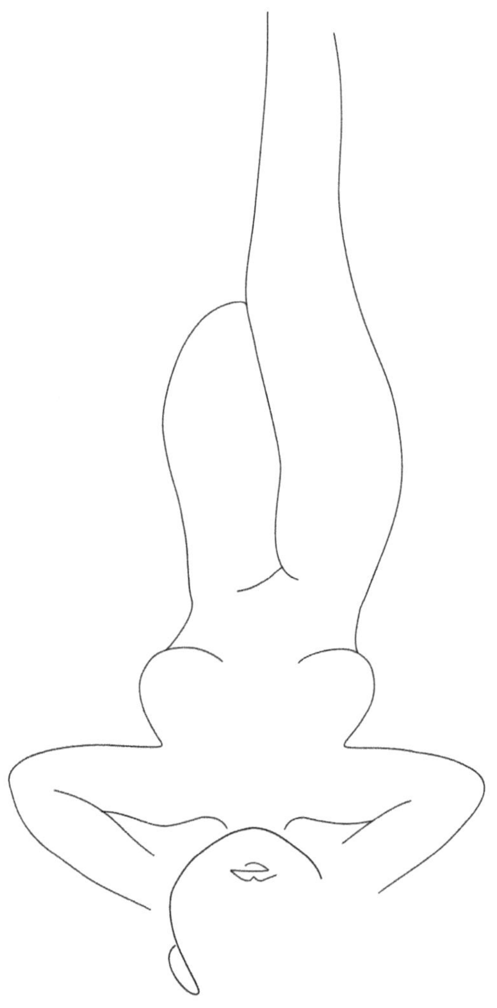

MALIGNANT ALLURE

You're my hemlock
Poisoning my philosophy
Breaking my forms and axioms,
For your form and figure

Your voice, a soothing sweet Malignant,
Soft to my ear,
Dark to my soul

Your frame, a cognitive biohazard,
Delicious to my senses,
Disorder to my spirit

Your eyes, an alluring acid,
Gentle gems of beauty
Corroding my emotions

Your essence a sensual disease

Savory to my sight and taste

Infecting my healthy being

You're my madness

Tender tepid tantalizing seductress

Encouraging my intrusive thoughts

To envelop your deepest spots

GREEN DRESS

"Lights, action
No camera because our eyes focused
      on one another when I came in.

I came out to forget about her,
You came out to look at someone besides him,
We don't have to be alone tonight.

We don't have to be perfect for each other.
Just for the moment
We don't have to be the next,
Just passion for the night

We dance and sobriety is a distant dream,
Your eyes open for something new
My eyes forgetting the old
The beat twirls us closer

The deeper the night
The deeper the embrace
The darker the light
The darker the intentions

You move your body in the green dress
    like divine vine
You in the green dress is a gleaming emerald gem
Your eyes fixate on where you want to be
Your hands hold what they can

I interlock our gaze allowing the enzyme of lust
    to sweat its function out
I hold to your frame appreciating the curves
    of your near bronze tone
I grab your hand one time to feel your intentions

We move like the light disappeared,
We touch like the public are unwanted spectators
We kiss one time zapping us into a locked reality

Close moments of passion,

Call us out of the mass of humanity.

That's when I hear your voice unfiltered,

The Romanian voice sucks the remaining purity

    out of my intention,

Leaving me to wonder your frame

    without the green dress

Devious intentions lead us to the realm of solitude,

The accent of your ancestors entice

    my composure into seduction.

We kiss like our lips longed to be felt again,

We kiss like our lips haven't had water in ages,

We kiss like our lips are tired of being apart

We touch like our hands never felt passion

We touch like our bodies didn't just create

    fiery friction

Our passions call out like a chant,

The rhythmic friction from our contact

The swaying of my necklace in making movement

    to embrace all of you

The vaulted ceiling receives our shadows

Our passion creates a temple of heated devotion,

The desire to hear your wailing chants consumes me,

The desire to feel your architecture pulls me

The desire to feel your lips envelops me,

But the very thing pulling me close is now a hindrance,

Green dress, the emerald that grabbed my attention,

Now a forcefield hindering

    the furious lust yearning out,

Green dress, the green light to the right moment

Now a hindrance to the fertile fragrance of your skin

Green dress, a green field of watered desire,

Now a Rubik's Cube needing blood

    to return to the cranium..."

ABOUT THE AUTHOR

Marshall A. Azir grew up in Georgia and lives in Huntsville, Alabama. He was a former mentor to aspiring youth poets, and is a self-published author of two   poetry books. After earning his M.A. in Theology, he taught math at the middle school and high school levels for several years before joining the Army.

A writer and visionary in spirit as well as in action, Azir's interests span an extensive range of subjects, from science to history to space travel. He's even created his own language.

Rather than see himself as chained to any particular field, Azir views himself as a natural explorer.

His next mission, is to build his own literary multiverse.

In his free time, he enjoys working out, watching movies, and getting his engineering juices flowing by tinkering with Legos.

CONTACT

Email
Azirofwhasssa@gmail.com

ISBN 979-8-8690-1658-4

9 798869 016584